CONTENTS

GRAB THESE!

Are you ready to create some amazing pictures? Wait a minute! Before you begin drawing, you will need a few important pieces of equipment.

PENS AND PENCILS

You can use a variety of drawing tools including pens, chalks, pencils and paints. But to begin with use an ordinary HB pencil.

PAPER

Use a clean sheet of paper for your final drawings. Scrap paper is useful and cheap for your practice work.

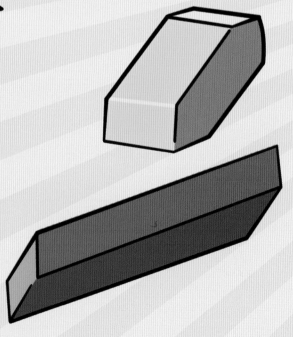

ERASERS

Everyone makes mistakes! That's why every artist has a good eraser. When you rub out a mistake, do it gently. Scrubbing hard at your paper will ruin your drawing and possibly even rip it.

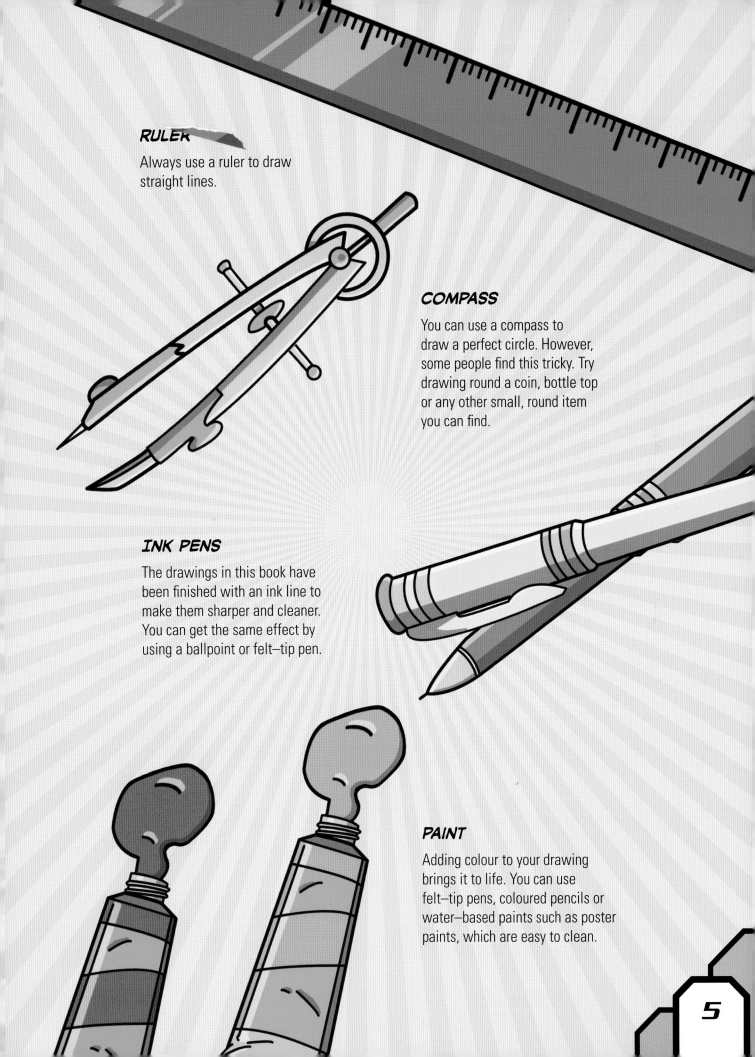

RULER

Always use a ruler to draw straight lines.

COMPASS

You can use a compass to draw a perfect circle. However, some people find this tricky. Try drawing round a coin, bottle top or any other small, round item you can find.

INK PENS

The drawings in this book have been finished with an ink line to make them sharper and cleaner. You can get the same effect by using a ballpoint or felt—tip pen.

PAINT

Adding colour to your drawing brings it to life. You can use felt—tip pens, coloured pencils or water—based paints such as poster paints, which are easy to clean.

GETTING STARTED

In this book we use a simple two-colour system to show you how to draw a picture. Just remember: new lines are blue lines!

STARTING WITH STEP 1

The first lines you will draw are very simple shapes. They will be shown in blue, like this. You should draw them with a normal HB pencil.

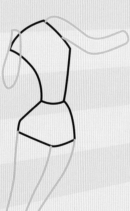

ADDING MORE DETAIL

As you move on to the next step, the lines you have already drawn will be shown in black. The new lines for that stage will appear in blue.

FINISHING YOUR PICTURE

When you reach the final stage you will see the image in full colour with a black ink line. Inking a picture means tracing the main lines with a black pen. After the ink dries, use your eraser to remove all the pencil lines before adding your colour.

LIGHT AND SHADE

If you want to make your picture look 3–D, start thinking about light and shade. Decide which side of your picture is in shadow, and make the colours darker along either the left or right edge. Just use a darker version of the colour you have already used in that area.

FELT--TIP PENS

You can create bold colours and strong lines with felt–tip pens. However, it's not easy to correct mistakes that you've made with a pen. So start off with a pencil sketch first! Add the felt–tip colours once you're happy with the result.

COLOURING PENCILS

These create a paler and calmer look than felt–tips. Colouring pencils are also easier to blend together. Sketch your drawing first with an HB pencil. Then, gently layer your colour, making it as light or as dark as you like.

WATERCOLOURS

Watercolours are easy to blend together and you can create beautiful pictures. First, sketch your drawing with a waterproof pen. Then, add water to your paint, but don't add too much. If you do, it might spoil your paper.

WOOD FAIRY

A wood fairy is a mischievous little person with magical powers. She has pointy ears like an elf and delicate wings that help her to flutter from tree to tree.

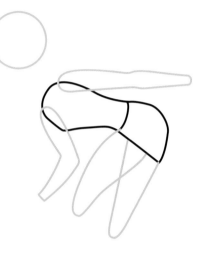

STEP 1

First, draw the shape above to make the main body of the fairy.

STEP 2

Next, add arms, legs and a simple circle to start the fairy's head.

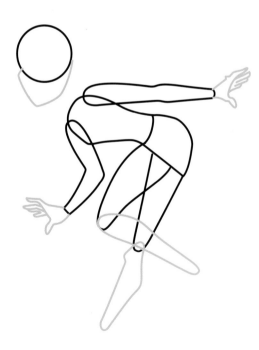

STEP 3

Draw a pointed shape on the circle for her chin. Carefully draw her hands and add her lower legs.

STEP 4

Now add her hair, a pointy ear, a neck and some feet. Her hair can be any style but this pixie cut looks best.

STEP 5

After you have added her clothes and face, draw on her beautiful fairy wings.

STEP 6

You can make your fairy any colour you want. Just remember that she has to look at home amongst flowers and trees.

9

FAIRYTALE PRINCESS

The fairytale princess wears a long, flowing gown and a golden crown. She looks happy, and her dress sparkles as if it's been sprinkled with fairy dust.

STEP 1

First, draw a stylish dress. Look at the way it curves out at the bottom.

STEP 2

Add a circle for her head and long, slender arms.

STEP 3

Carefully draw her hands and add a pointed chin.

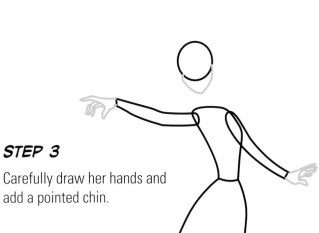

STEP 4

Add her feet, a big bow, puffy sleeves, more details and then her crown. Draw her long hair, ear and neck. Add the little bird.

STEP 5

Finish her pretty face, shoes and the little bird. Then, add more details to the dress as shown.

STEP 6

Time to add colour! We've chosen blue but you could use any colour.

SUPER TIP!

An easy way to add sparkle to the princess's dress is to leave small dots of the picture without colour.

Another way to make the small white sparkles is to add little dots of white poster paint.

Keep them spread out – don't bunch them up in one place.

SKY FAIRY

Sky fairies spend their days playing hide–and–seek in the clouds. These fairies have soft, rounded wings and they even look a bit like fluffy clouds.

STEP 1

First, draw two shapes that look like a lower–case letter 'i'.

STEP 2

Add her arms, chin and her floaty cloud skirt.

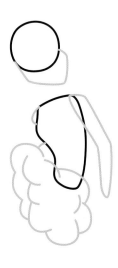

STEP 3

Carefully add her hand and the top of her legs.

STEP 4

Finish off her legs, then draw her mouth and ear. Add a big, fluffy hairstyle, rather like candyfloss!

STEP 5

Now it's time to add her eyes and her other hand. Soft, rounded wings complete the picture.

SUPER TIP!

It's very easy to change the sky fairy into a storm fairy, just by changing the colours of her clothes, hair and face.

We've used dark blue and purple to make her a storm fairy. Why don't you use other colours to make her into another type of fairy?

STEP 6

She could be a bright sky fairy like this one. Or you could use darker colours to make her a storm fairy. See the Super Tip on the left.

PIRATE PRINCESS

Our pirate princess may not wear a long dress, but her golden crown and purple clothes show that she's real royalty!

STEP 1

This wonky outline is the main body shape.

STEP 2

Add a head and then the tops of her arms and legs.

STEP 3

Draw her arms, hands and lower legs. Then add her chin and a line across her forehead for her crown.

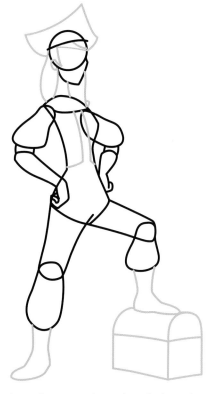

STEP 4

Add chunky pirate boots and a pointed pirate hat. Don't forget her chest of precious jewels.

STEP 5

Add her waistcoat and crown, a belt and big hoop earrings. Give the treasure chest more detail. The eye patch completes her look!

STEP 6

Colour her in with bold shades. We've used purple but you can use any of your favourite colours. Make her crown nice and shiny.

FLAME FAIRY

Bright red hair, flaming wings and an orange dress tell you that this fairy is hot stuff. She really looks like she's made of fire!

STEP 1

First, draw the top of her dress and then add her fire skirt. Use pointy shapes to give it movement.

STEP 2

Next, add a circle for her head. Then, draw her long arms and the top parts of her legs.

STEP 3

Now add a pointy chin and a hand. Finish her legs.

STEP 4

Add her ears, flaming hair, wings and pointy feet.

STEP 5

Now draw her face and add
some simple lines
for her dress and shoes.

STEP 6

Choose hot colours like orange
and red to make a flame fairy.
Use shades of blue and white if
you want to make an ice fairy.

NATIVE AMERICAN PRINCESS

This Native American princess wears her traditional dress with pride. Decorate her outfit with plenty of tassels and feathers.

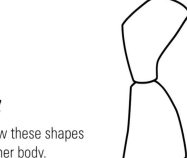

STEP 1

First, draw these shapes to make her body.

STEP 2

Next, add a circle for her head. Draw her arms and the tops of her legs.

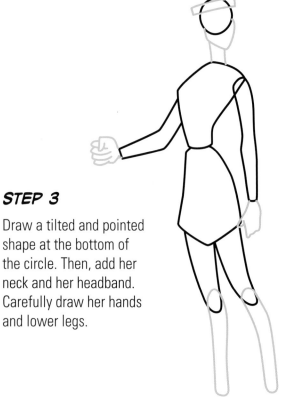

STEP 3

Draw a tilted and pointed shape at the bottom of the circle. Then, add her neck and her headband. Carefully draw her hands and lower legs.

STEP 4

Add the staff, her hair, her cuffs and her feet. Her dress needs a little more detail too.

STEP 5

Draw feathers on her staff and her headband. Add lots of fringing to her dress. Finish her face and shoes.

STEP 6

Her clothes are made from animal skins, but you could decorate them with fabulous jewels if you want to.

EXPLORER FAIRY

The explorer fairy loves adventure. With her hat, gloves, goggles and a map in her hand, she's always ready to discover new places.

STEP 1

First, draw a curvy shape for her body.

STEP 2

Next, draw her arms. The arm on the left should point up. Add a head and legs.

STEP 3

Add her chin. Then draw her hands, bringing the left one up to her chin. Add a neck and big eyes. Then finish her legs.

STEP 4

Now draw the goggles and add long straps to her helmet. Next, add her wings, gloves and hair.

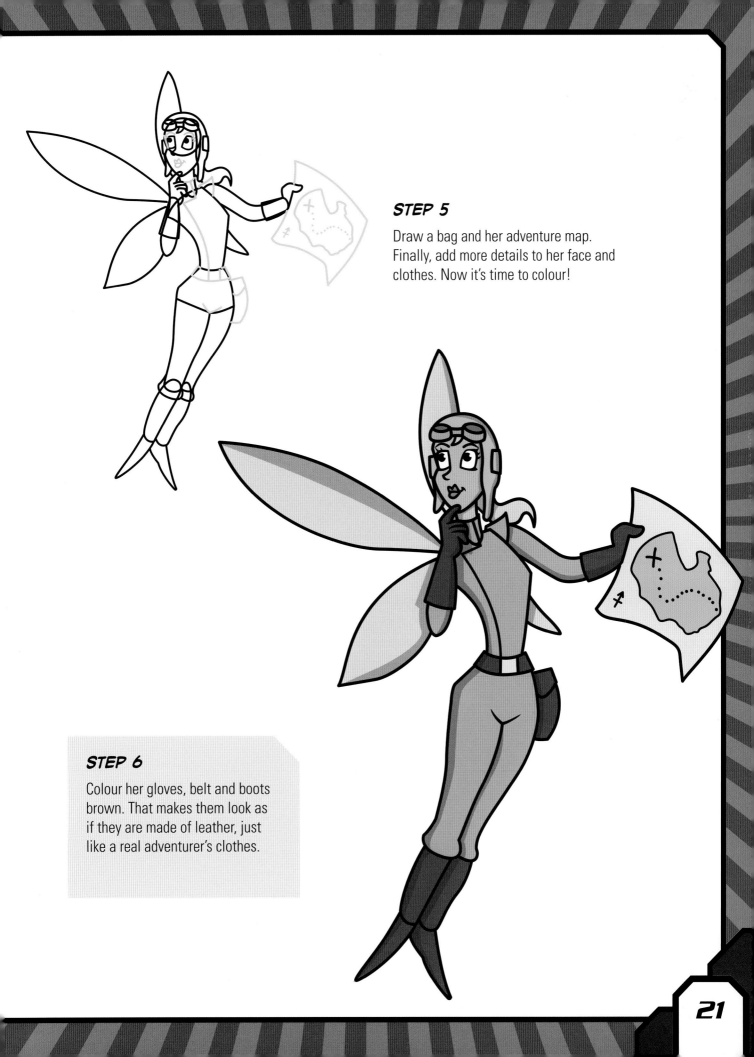

STEP 5

Draw a bag and her adventure map. Finally, add more details to her face and clothes. Now it's time to colour!

STEP 6

Colour her gloves, belt and boots brown. That makes them look as if they are made of leather, just like a real adventurer's clothes.

AFRICAN PRINCESS

This African princess wears a simple dress with bright colours. Her pretty jewels and feathered headband make her look truly royal.

STEP 1

Start by drawing her long dress to make a simple body shape.

STEP 2

Now add her head, long neck and arms to give her a royal look.

STEP 3

Add her pointed chin, her hands and her bare feet.

STEP 4

Draw her pretty headband
with its feathers. Add her
earrings, cuffs and a fold
in her dress.

STEP 5

Now draw her face and
necklace, and add the
stripes to her dress.

STEP 6

Use bright colours to help this
princess pop off the page!

FAIRY GODMOTHER

A fairy godmother is always ready to help people. She'll use her fairy wings and trusty magic wand to sort out any problem.

STEP 1

Use these two round shapes to begin her body.

STEP 2

Add a circle for her head and draw her arms.

STEP 3

Draw her hair and face. Her hands and little legs come next.

STEP 4

She needs some fairy wings, so that she can take flight. Don't forget that magic wand!

STEP 5

Finish her face. Then, top the wand with a magic star and add a shawl over her shoulders.

STEP 6

Choose friendly, bold colours for your fairy godmother. You can always add some sparkles if you want to.

SUPER TIP!

Add some sparkles to your fairy's magic wand to show how magical it is.

- A very simple way to make sparkles is to draw a small group of shapes like these circles and stars.

- Sprinkle the sparkly shapes around the wand. Some of them can trail behind the wand to show how it is moving.

ARABIAN PRINCESS

This Arabian princess looks fabulous in her pink two–piece outfit and sparkling jewels. She is ready to take a trip on a magic carpet!

STEP 1

First, draw a simple body shape made up of trousers and a top.

STEP 2

Next, add an oval shape for her head. Then draw her arms and feet.

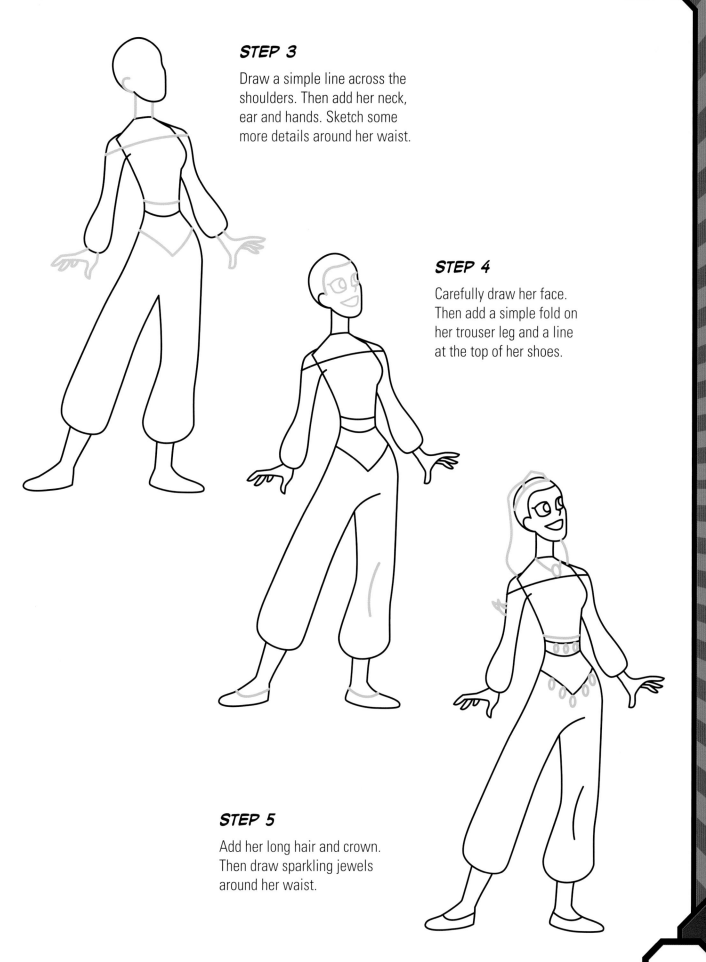

STEP 3

Draw a simple line across the shoulders. Then add her neck, ear and hands. Sketch some more details around her waist.

STEP 4

Carefully draw her face. Then add a simple fold on her trouser leg and a line at the top of her shoes.

STEP 5

Add her long hair and crown. Then draw sparkling jewels around her waist.

We've coloured her outfit in shades of pink. You could even add a magic carpet.

This fairy loves bright colours. Even her skirt is like a beautiful rainbow. With a wave of her magic wand, she paints all across the sky.

STEP 1

First, draw a simple shape for her curved skirt and top.

STEP 2

Next, draw her head, slightly tilted. Draw a bent leg, a straight leg and then her arms.

STEP 3

Now, sketch in her fluttering wings and carefully draw her hands.

STEP 4

Add feet, hair, dress detail and a magic wand.

STEP 5

Now finish her face. Then add the rainbow. You could trace around a cup to get the curve just right.

STEP 6

Time to colour. Remember, she's a rainbow fairy... so use as many different colours as possible!

GLOSSARY

3--D Three–dimensional. A 3-D object has height, width and depth, like an object in the real world.

chunky Heavy and thick.

cuff The end part of a sleeve, around the wrist.

elf A creature from folk tales with pointed ears and magical powers.

HB pencil A pencil that is neither soft not hard, but something in between.

pixie A mischievous, playful elf or fairy.

poster paint A water–based, bright–coloured paint often used for posters.

tassel A bunch of loose threads that are bound at one end, used as a decoration on curtains or clothes.

watercolour An artist's paint that is thinned with water to give it a transparent quality.

wonky Uneven.

FURTHER READING

How to Draw Fairies by David Antram (Bookhouse, 2011)

How to Draw Fairies and Mermaids by Fiona Watt (Usborne Publishing , 2013)

Junior How to Draw Fairies by Kate Thompson (Top That!, 2011)

WEBSITES

fairytownlove.weebly.com/index.html

www.disney.co.uk/disney–fairies/games

www.educationalcoloringpages.com/fairy.html

INDEX